MW00929706

THIS BOOK BELONGS TO:

_____

SCHOOL YEAR: _____

Copyright © 2019 by 365 Teacher Resources & Prints

All rights reserved. No part of this publication may be reproduced, distributed, or transmitted in any form or by any means, including photocopying, recording, or other electronic or mechanical methods, without the prior written permission of the publisher, except in the case of brief quotations embodied in critical reviews and certain other noncommercial uses permitted by copyright law.

RTI STUDENT *List*

NAME	TIER	SUBJECT	NOTES

RTI STUDENT *List*

NAME	TIER	SUBJECT	NOTES

RTI - INTERVENTION Groups

GROUP: .... TIER: .... SUBJECT: ....

STUDENTS:

1. ....
2. ....
3. ....

4. ....
5. ....
6. ....

NOTES: ....
....
....
....
....

GROUP: .... TIER: .... SUBJECT: ....

STUDENTS:

1. ....
2. ....
3. ....

4. ....
5. ....
6. ....

NOTES: ....
....
....
....
....

RTI - INTERVENTION *Groups*

GROUP: .... TIER: .... SUBJECT: ....

STUDENTS:

1. ....
2. ....
3. ....

4. ....
5. ....
6. ....

NOTES: ....
....
....
....
....

GROUP: .... TIER: .... SUBJECT: ....

STUDENTS:

1. ....
2. ....
3. ....

4. ....
5. ....
6. ....

NOTES: ....
....
....
....
....

RTI - INTERVENTION *Groups*

GROUP: _____ TIER: _____ SUBJECT: _____

STUDENTS:

1. _____ 4. _____

2. _____ 5. _____

3. _____ 6. _____

NOTES:

_____

_____

_____

_____

GROUP: _____ TIER: _____ SUBJECT: _____

STUDENTS:

1. _____ 4. _____

2. _____ 5. _____

3. _____ 6. _____

NOTES:

_____

_____

_____

_____

RTI STUDENT *Profile*

NAME: TEACHER:

GRADE: START DATE:

| AREA OF CONCERN: *READING* ◯   *MATH* ◯ | TIER: 2   3 |

TARGET AREA

GOAL(S)

INTERVENTION

INTERVENTIONIST

FREQUENCY/DURATION

RESULTS & OBSERVATIONS

PROGRESS MONITORING *Data*

NAME: _____   SUBJECT: _____

DATE	ASSESSMENT	SCORE	NOTES

PROGRESS MONITORING Data

NAME: _____   SUBJECT: _____

DATE	ASSESSMENT	SCORE	NOTES

PROGRESS MONITORING *Data*

NAME: _____   SUBJECT: _____

DATE	ASSESSMENT	SCORE	NOTES

RTI STUDENT *Profile*

NAME: TEACHER:

GRADE: START DATE:

AREA OF CONCERN: *READING* ◯   *MATH* ◯ | TIER: 2   3

TARGET AREA

GOAL(S)

INTERVENTION

INTERVENTIONIST

FREQUENCY/DURATION

RESULTS & OBSERVATIONS

PROGRESS MONITORING *Data*

NAME: _____   SUBJECT: _____

DATE	ASSESSMENT	SCORE	NOTES

PROGRESS MONITORING *Data*

NAME: _____   SUBJECT: _____

DATE	ASSESSMENT	SCORE	NOTES

PROGRESS MONITORING Data

NAME: _____   SUBJECT: _____

DATE	ASSESSMENT	SCORE	NOTES

RTI STUDENT *Profile*

NAME:	TEACHER:
GRADE:	START DATE:

AREA OF CONCERN: *READING* ◯ *MATH* ◯	TIER: 2 3

TARGET AREA

GOAL(S)

INTERVENTION

INTERVENTIONIST

FREQUENCY/DURATION

RESULTS & OBSERVATIONS

PROGRESS MONITORING Data

NAME: _____   SUBJECT: _____

DATE	ASSESSMENT	SCORE	NOTES

PROGRESS MONITORING Data

NAME: _____   SUBJECT: _____

DATE	ASSESSMENT	SCORE	NOTES

PROGRESS MONITORING *Data*

NAME: _____   SUBJECT: _____

DATE	ASSESSMENT	SCORE	NOTES

RTI STUDENT *Profile*

NAME: TEACHER:

GRADE: START DATE:

AREA OF CONCERN: *READING* ◯   *MATH* ◯   TIER: 2   3

TARGET AREA

GOAL(S)

INTERVENTION

INTERVENTIONIST

FREQUENCY/DURATION

RESULTS & OBSERVATIONS

PROGRESS MONITORING *Data*

NAME: _____   SUBJECT: _____

DATE	ASSESSMENT	SCORE	NOTES

PROGRESS MONITORING *Data*

NAME: _____   SUBJECT: _____

DATE	ASSESSMENT	SCORE	NOTES

PROGRESS MONITORING *Data*

NAME: _____   SUBJECT: _____

DATE	ASSESSMENT	SCORE	NOTES

RTI STUDENT *Profile*

NAME: TEACHER:

GRADE: START DATE:

AREA OF CONCERN: *READING* ◯   *MATH* ◯   TIER: 2   3

TARGET AREA

GOAL(S)

INTERVENTION

INTERVENTIONIST

FREQUENCY/DURATION

RESULTS & OBSERVATIONS

PROGRESS MONITORING Data

NAME: _____   SUBJECT: _____

DATE	ASSESSMENT	SCORE	NOTES

PROGRESS MONITORING *Data*

NAME: _____   SUBJECT: _____

DATE	ASSESSMENT	SCORE	NOTES

PROGRESS MONITORING *Data*

NAME: _____   SUBJECT: _____

DATE	ASSESSMENT	SCORE	NOTES

RTI STUDENT *Profile*

NAME: TEACHER:

GRADE: START DATE:

AREA OF CONCERN: *READING* ◯   *MATH* ◯   TIER: 2   3

TARGET AREA

GOAL(S)

INTERVENTION

INTERVENTIONIST

FREQUENCY/DURATION

RESULTS & OBSERVATIONS

PROGRESS MONITORING Data

NAME: _____   SUBJECT: _____

DATE	ASSESSMENT	SCORE	NOTES

PROGRESS MONITORING *Data*

NAME: _____   SUBJECT: _____

DATE	ASSESSMENT	SCORE	NOTES

PROGRESS MONITORING *Data*

NAME: _____   SUBJECT: _____

DATE	ASSESSMENT	SCORE	NOTES

RTI STUDENT *Profile*

NAME: TEACHER:

GRADE: START DATE:

AREA OF CONCERN: *READING* ◯   *MATH* ◯   TIER: 2   3

TARGET AREA

GOAL(S)

INTERVENTION

INTERVENTIONIST

FREQUENCY/DURATION

RESULTS & OBSERVATIONS

PROGRESS MONITORING Data

NAME: _____   SUBJECT: _____

DATE	ASSESSMENT	SCORE	NOTES

PROGRESS MONITORING Data

NAME: _____   SUBJECT: _____

DATE	ASSESSMENT	SCORE	NOTES

PROGRESS MONITORING *Data*

NAME: _____   SUBJECT: _____

DATE	ASSESSMENT	SCORE	NOTES

RTI STUDENT *Profile*

NAME: TEACHER:

GRADE: START DATE:

AREA OF CONCERN: *READING* ◯   *MATH* ◯ | TIER: 2   3

TARGET AREA

GOAL(S)

INTERVENTION

INTERVENTIONIST

FREQUENCY/DURATION

RESULTS & OBSERVATIONS

PROGRESS MONITORING Data

NAME: _____   SUBJECT: _____

DATE	ASSESSMENT	SCORE	NOTES

PROGRESS MONITORING Data

NAME: _____   SUBJECT: _____

DATE	ASSESSMENT	SCORE	NOTES

PROGRESS MONITORING Data

NAME: _____   SUBJECT: _____

DATE	ASSESSMENT	SCORE	NOTES

RTI STUDENT *Profile*

NAME:	TEACHER:
GRADE:	START DATE:

AREA OF CONCERN: *READING* ◯   *MATH* ◯   TIER: 2   3

TARGET AREA

GOAL(S)

INTERVENTION

INTERVENTIONIST

FREQUENCY/DURATION

RESULTS & OBSERVATIONS

PROGRESS MONITORING Data

NAME: _____   SUBJECT: _____

DATE	ASSESSMENT	SCORE	NOTES

PROGRESS MONITORING *Data*

NAME: _____   SUBJECT: _____

DATE	ASSESSMENT	SCORE	NOTES

PROGRESS MONITORING Data

NAME: _____   SUBJECT: _____

DATE	ASSESSMENT	SCORE	NOTES

RTI STUDENT *Profile*

NAME: TEACHER:

GRADE: START DATE:

AREA OF CONCERN: *READING* ◯   *MATH* ◯   TIER: 2   3

TARGET AREA

GOAL(S)

INTERVENTION

INTERVENTIONIST

FREQUENCY/DURATION

RESULTS & OBSERVATIONS

PROGRESS MONITORING *Data*

NAME: _____   SUBJECT: _____

DATE	ASSESSMENT	SCORE	NOTES

PROGRESS MONITORING *Data*

NAME: _____   SUBJECT: _____

DATE	ASSESSMENT	SCORE	NOTES

PROGRESS MONITORING Data

NAME: _____   SUBJECT: _____

DATE	ASSESSMENT	SCORE	NOTES

RTI STUDENT *Profile*

NAME: TEACHER:

GRADE: START DATE:

AREA OF CONCERN: *READING* ◯   *MATH* ◯   TIER: 2   3

TARGET AREA

GOAL(S)

INTERVENTION

INTERVENTIONIST

FREQUENCY/DURATION

RESULTS & OBSERVATIONS

PROGRESS MONITORING *Data*

NAME: _____   SUBJECT: _____

DATE	ASSESSMENT	SCORE	NOTES

PROGRESS MONITORING Data

NAME: _____   SUBJECT: _____

DATE	ASSESSMENT	SCORE	NOTES

PROGRESS MONITORING Data

NAME: _____ SUBJECT: _____

DATE	ASSESSMENT	SCORE	NOTES

RTI STUDENT *Profile*

NAME: TEACHER:

GRADE: START DATE:

AREA OF CONCERN: *READING* ◯   *MATH* ◯   TIER: 2   3

TARGET AREA

GOAL(S)

INTERVENTION

INTERVENTIONIST

FREQUENCY/DURATION

RESULTS & OBSERVATIONS

PROGRESS MONITORING Data

NAME: _____   SUBJECT: _____

DATE	ASSESSMENT	SCORE	NOTES

PROGRESS MONITORING *Data*

NAME: _____   SUBJECT: _____

DATE	ASSESSMENT	SCORE	NOTES

PROGRESS MONITORING Data

NAME: _____   SUBJECT: _____

DATE	ASSESSMENT	SCORE	NOTES

RTI STUDENT *Profile*

NAME: TEACHER:

GRADE: START DATE:

AREA OF CONCERN: *READING* ◯   *MATH* ◯   TIER: 2   3

TARGET AREA

GOAL(S)

INTERVENTION

INTERVENTIONIST

FREQUENCY/DURATION

RESULTS & OBSERVATIONS

PROGRESS MONITORING Data

NAME: _____   SUBJECT: _____

DATE	ASSESSMENT	SCORE	NOTES

PROGRESS MONITORING Data

NAME: _____   SUBJECT: _____

DATE	ASSESSMENT	SCORE	NOTES

PROGRESS MONITORING *Data*

NAME: _____   SUBJECT: _____

DATE	ASSESSMENT	SCORE	NOTES

RTI STUDENT *Profile*

NAME:

TEACHER:

GRADE:

START DATE:

AREA OF CONCERN: *READING* ◯ *MATH* ◯ | TIER: 2 3

TARGET AREA

GOAL(S)

INTERVENTION

INTERVENTIONIST

FREQUENCY/DURATION

RESULTS & OBSERVATIONS

PROGRESS MONITORING Data

NAME: _____   SUBJECT: _____

DATE	ASSESSMENT	SCORE	NOTES

PROGRESS MONITORING Data

NAME: _____   SUBJECT: _____

DATE	ASSESSMENT	SCORE	NOTES

PROGRESS MONITORING Data

NAME: _____   SUBJECT: _____

DATE	ASSESSMENT	SCORE	NOTES

RTI STUDENT *Profile*

NAME: TEACHER:

GRADE: START DATE:

AREA OF CONCERN: *READING* ◯ *MATH* ◯   TIER: 2   3

TARGET AREA

GOAL(S)

INTERVENTION

INTERVENTIONIST

FREQUENCY/DURATION

RESULTS & OBSERVATIONS

PROGRESS MONITORING *Data*

NAME: _____   SUBJECT: _____

DATE	ASSESSMENT	SCORE	NOTES

PROGRESS MONITORING *Data*

NAME: _____   SUBJECT: _____

DATE	ASSESSMENT	SCORE	NOTES

PROGRESS MONITORING *Data*

NAME: _____   SUBJECT: _____

DATE	ASSESSMENT	SCORE	NOTES

Thank you!

For enquiries and feedback, please email us:

365teacherresources@gmail.com

Made in the USA
Middletown, DE
10 October 2020

21406730R00055